My First Animal Library

Beavers

by Mari Schuh

Bullfrog Books

Ideas for Parents and Teachers

Bullfrog Books let children practice reading informational text at the earliest reading levels. Repetition, familiar words, and photo labels support early readers.

Before Reading

- Discuss the cover photo. What does it tell them?
- Look at the picture glossary together. Read and discuss the words.

Read the Book

- "Walk" through the book and look at the photos. Let the child ask questions. Point out the photo labels.
- Read the book to the child, or have him or her read independently.

After Reading

- Prompt the child to think more. Ask: Have you built a fort that's like a beaver's lodge? Did you work hard like a beaver to make it?

Bullfrog Books are published by Jump!
5357 Penn Avenue South
Minneapolis, MN 55419
www.jumplibrary.com

Library of Congress Cataloging-in-Publication Data

Schuh, Mari C., 1975–author.
  Beavers / by Mari Schuh.
     pages cm.—(My first animal library)
  "Bullfrog Books are published by Jump!."
  Audience: Age 5.
  Audience: K to grade 3.
  Includes index.
  ISBN 978-1-62031-173-8 (hardcover)
  ISBN 978-1-62496-260-8 (ebook)
  1. Beavers—Juvenile literature. I. Title.
  QL737.R632S38 2015
  599.37—dc23
                                      2014037207

Series Editor: Wendy Dieker
Series Designer: Ellen Huber
Book Designer: Lindaanne Donohoe
Photo Researcher: Michelle Sonnek

Photo Credits: Age Fotostock, 14–15; Alamy, 5; Biosphoto, 18–19; Corbis, 20–21; Getty, cover, 1, 3, 22; iStock, 6–7, 23bl; Science Source Images, 17; Shutterstock, 4, 11, 16; SuperStock, 6, 8–9, 10, 12–13, 14, 23tl, 23br, 23tr, 24.

Printed in the United States of America at Corporate Graphics in North Mankato, Minnesota.

For David and Alex. —MS

Table of Contents

Busy Beavers 4

Parts of a Beaver 22

Picture Glossary 23

Index 24

To Learn More 24

Busy Beavers

Beavers are hard at work.

Why?

They are making a dam.

The beavers gnaw wood with their sharp teeth.

They cut down trees.

teeth

The beavers pull logs
to a river.

They pull branches, too.

They add mud and rocks.

All done!

Look!

A pond forms.

Now the beavers make a home.

It is called a lodge.

They use sticks, plants, and mud.

lodge

Oh, no!
A wolf!

16

Slap! Slap!

A beaver hits his tail on the water.

He warns others.

lodge
entrance

18

Splash!

The beavers dive
under the water.

They swim to the lodge.

Now they are safe.
They rest in their
warm home.

Parts of a Beaver

fur
A beaver's waterproof fur keeps it warm and dry.

eyes
Beavers have small eyes and can't see well.

tail
A beaver's wide, flat tail helps it steer when it swims.

webbed feet
Webbed back feet help beavers swim.

Picture Glossary

dam
A wall that beavers make across streams and rivers to hold back water.

lodge
A beaver's home.

gnaw
To chew and wear away bit by bit.

pond
A small body of water.

Index

dam 5

home 14, 20

lodge 14, 19

mud 10, 14

pond 13

river 9

tail 17

teeth 6

trees 6

water 17, 19

To Learn More

Learning more is as easy as 1, 2, 3.

1) Go to www.factsurfer.com

2) Enter "beavers" into the search box.

3) Click the "Surf" button to see a list of websites.

With factsurfer.com, finding more information is just a click away.

24